The author was born in Scarborough where he lives again now after spending time in London and various regions of the UK, as well as abroad in Denmark. France, Cyprus, the USA and Australia. He has worked for Customs and Excise and in the Royal Air Force and the Royal Mail, along with various jobs in book shops, farms and factories.

He has made documentary films, translated French books, published poems and stories in small press. He has had painting exhibitions in several countries.

DEDICATION

To Michael Henry (1943-2021)

Patrick Henry

A VIRUS IN WRY VERSE

A Poem Sequence

AUSTIN MACAULEY PUBLISHERS™

LONDON • CAMBRIDGE • NEW YORK • SHARJAH

A CIP catalogue record for this title is available from the British Library.

ISBN 9781398414761 (Paperback)
ISBN 9781398414747 (ePub e-book)

www.austinmacauley.com

First Published (2021)
Austin Macauley Publishers Ltd
25 Canada Square
Canary Wharf
London
E14 5LQ

POEMS

Planet Taking Pains

In downpour seasons, wild rivers flood low towns.
Households swept to rooftops, miss lost possessions.
From Ganges to Mecca: faith zeal wells too deep.
Lives crushed in haste, where eternal hopes build up.

Rhino, Zebra, Impala: run the gauntlet, kills beat down.
Nature's balance tilts. Human aims threaten.
Their skills reached a summit, to split the nuclear.
Powers made boundless: spread alarm to the force of war,

Test Ban Treaties caused checks, to level the vast threat.
Now, fuel outputs raise dust clouds that soil the world.
Plastic waste clogs seas: gnaws doubts and coral reefs.
Whales strain to breathe through mist huge as ocean heaves.

Under the microscope, one viral speck
Appears like a crown, whose glinting points can break
Through body defence: an unknown potent germ:
Grown a strange flawed streak from a wild food chain.

From China to the West: victims given intense care,
Strive to live through lockdowns of nations, where,
Streets bare, stores shut: restless sorts look flying nowhere:
As rare threatened birds, stay close, until the coast is clear.

China Dish Breaking

Three decades back: I'd sailed round Yangtze-side towns.
Meals served to diners: the most bizarre they'd seen.
Head parts, offal, down to the feet and bones.
Wuhan markets, start this strange lethal, food chain.

An Orient mix stirred to the boiling point.
Eye of newt, toe of frog, wool of bat, tongue of dog.
Macbeth cauldron-chants, witches intoned:
Recipe for disaster, filed in a far travel's log:

Delivered longer than most Chinese takeaways.
Chop Suey started on stoves near Brooklyn long-shore wharves.
Ordered to universal taste, found widely, nowadays
Unknown: where life on the bare Yellow River starves.

Reduced to gorging on diets: gruesome, stark,
Poison passed from night bat to jackal or pangolin.
Innards from all paired creatures marched into The Ark,
Corona Virus, lands unseen. Its deadly fangs sink in.

The Deepest Toll in Rajasthan

The slow train slurs to a complete halt,
From steady, careful progress, passed each day:
Bearing millions in a safe, broad, generous hold.
Bringing vast wealth of character varied in each way.

Nights long gladly known to give alert sense:
Travelling through huge, calm, half-sleeping land.
Snaking along inside, comradeship builds down trains.
Bursting from night's tunnel: fresh daylight newly found.

Rail India: employs six million souls.
Transports millions through each hour in twenty-four.
In seated order. Not packed in the wild squalor:
False news in slanted pictures, slyly tells.

Crowds will gather in dense mass round the Ganges;
At Kumbh Mela: the great Hindu holy feast.
As pilgrim routes can take grave toll from wild chances.
One stays thankful: last year, no life they lost.

Railways stop. Corona Virus blocks our tracks.
Lives at threat. Worst count, in Bhilwara, textile town,
Sounds like a strict, heeded warning: tightly spun.
Amid hazards the land endures. This last Virus, aches.

From Heel to Head in Italy

This Corona figure: proved drastic being let in,
Among those drawn before, to the gates of Milan.
Medici mercers: proud in silk, power, finance.
Then, tough Borgias, came to oust this fine balance.
The Bari clan: robust from the hungry South.
Skilled at Ring-craft and crime such fight brings forth.
In the Rocco film: epic of hard struggled tragedy,
Gripped crowds: how prize-fighters stage their grim story:
Blow by blow, beats down a rich, corrupt city.
This grainy film spilled one last drop of pity.

Now fine as silk, these threads worm, flawed, from The East
Virus prongs through flesh and lungs, of the human cast,
Who parade this suave fashion and wealth-capital,
Where swamp-creek crocodile skin, gives smart, total
Sheen to the high style in leisurewear.
A place bathed in sun, until dark clouds show fear,
The danger, now, bulks large: but minute, on the horizon.
Vast lives at risk. News hard and bitter to swallow down.

Bergamot Quells Tastes of Anxiety

Bergamo knew unjust dense trouble before.
In Quasimodo's poem: prisoners of war,
Held in the town's fort of huge, iced-up walls.
Down deep dark cells where no light falls:
They think of deer and heron, who roam freely past
These bars, like sad cypress branches: iron-cast.
Shouts from guards, anger those locked down the jail:
Who grieve for young comrades, lost in the brutal kill.

Bergamot lightens harsh tastes: black bitter tea leaves.
In this new lockdown: minds know, this measure saves
Lives, if kept from the slight, but fatal touch,
Corona Virus could stretch across to reach.
Days, nights: once more: closed silent as that hated prison:
The poet; dramatised: to speak for intense passion.

The Peril Arena in Castile

Goya, strangely self-locked into their rich domain
To draw sublime satire from the Bourbon-Parma crown.
Paid by them, working in that palatial home:
He'd relish irony, should Corona Virus come.

Under the skin: his Black Arts slid sinister traits;
In The Prado, his line descending from Art Greats.
Velasquez, viewing the infantas and meninas, strange pride.
From Murillo, Ribera: taking the dark, hungry side.

Through Goya's own portrayals of anger, passion, infamy.
The 1808 executions. The betrayal at Gethsemane.
To the legacy in Picasso's vast mockery, through *Guernica*,
Where genocide, great art, and sarcasm: occur.

Across Madrid, skirls of matador, screams of dying bulls,
Reach crescendo. Flamenco chords and skirts raise high thrills.
Lorca's drama and poems, stir Left voices: or Franco's fears,
By different ways. The poet, like most resisters, disappears.

Fascist leaders sent Blitz planes and murderous troops.
The Fifth Column phrase, coined: would dash last brave hopes.
A city on the hill: El Greco showed rise through dense clouds;
Now fights the Virus, alone. Dispersed from raging crowds.

Time in Athens

Freshly arrived here, mostly to breathe in
A sense of calm reason, reached through time
Existing before the rise of creeds or war upheavals
Broke that fine web, where whole thought reveals.
Strange, learning how that need for the Renaissance,
Delved from studies which dug through ruined Athens.
Culture revived, that the fearing Dark Ages, lost.
Most great art since, might not have surfaced.
Nor reason and verbal skills, which enlighten
Where doubt and suspicion, darkly maintain.
Light of Athens, reflected like precious stones;
Science and meaning, debated wide at meetings,
Forbidden now this Virus scare shuts down
Gatherings of worth, the Greeks had deeply woven.
The book I bought, showed Plato on the cover.
Debating with Socrates, on the world all over.
Aristotle seen further entering the picture.
All like the wise Magi, beneath a guiding star.
Minds think, this plague now harshly visiting:
Caused, by our centre's lost hold, in polluting.

The Seine Can Act Wild

Hard to think of Paris near closed down once more.
Suave cafes, most times: sparkling day and night till dawn.
But for that harsh curfew enforced in the '40s war.
I moved there later, when tense streets could warn:
Fire of dissent that stoked revolt, might still erupt
From the mouth: red and angry, in the young.
Against control through means unequal and corrupt.
Rebel cries and songs sound thrilling in the Gallic tongue
Liaisons in love, Left politics, police affairs:
Weave through the town, down ways of intrigue, unseen.
Such guile used to drastic effect: now deserves,
To counter threats from this unknown, lethal Virus strain.

Checkpoint Recall at Berlin

A schizoid case could be made out for this city:
Split decades through ashes: war defeat left strewed.
Crashed huge as Crystal Night stays sharp in the harsh story:
Starting to this dead end down a long divided road.
By the Brandenburg Gate, one dreams, hearing Bach played:
Fine as taut strings: bowed by victims in the death-camp band.
The final solution led to the last judgement made,
At Nuremberg: on which the Reich's insane defence, once hanged.
Berlin, no more capital. Wealth and power all spent.
Russian might: wrenched it to zones: West or East.
Now returned whole, as the head town in its full state.
The Cold War Red Curtain, rolling back, at last.
Traffic flows fugue rhythms through Brandenburg Gate.
Corona Virus, now the challenge, at the next checkpoint.

The Concert of Vienna

A place which tells of the Venus-aura, trailed through woods.
A touch of love, dancing down light-hearted moods,
In piano music, spread out to run through crisp tones:
Or heard in wispy sighs from vague, long-horned gramophones.
More heavy minds, value the sound tread
Of sonata composers, fitting most perfect in each key.
Or else, treasure fine arts, of Klimt, Schiele and Klee:
And labyrinths of the mind, Freud and Jung explore.
Unknown, the young artist Adolf: they rejected here:
Back, later, he seized their country in his power.
And annexed without mercy: half the world over.
Corona Virus, now also tilts a shadow at this door;
Growing vast and lethal, as times his jackboots strode.
Haunts of genius, like this place: might know the right answer.

Silence Over Ice-Cold Steppes

From Red Square: no move never means no threat
Arrives or exits at this nerve centre spot.
In chess: that Castle move. Their Kremlin hides their King:
A figure of high power in his cold Presidium.
At the start, their Press called *Pravda* and *Izvestia*:
Meant the Truth and the Spark of revolt's fire.
News, blank: first speaks no sign of Virus here.
Underground sounds hint: Corona lurks there.
Remains of the Crown, they swept off the board,
A monarch shape there: speaks for the People's word.
Breaks silence: his land admits these flaws exist.
Still playing all the ace cards, close to the chest.

Fears on the Waterfront

New York. The scare came late, but builds up fast.
Broadway's White Way, weaves a show round deadly ills,
Which flesh can turn corrupt from. So, at last,
The ending makes good from great content and wild thrills.

Strong books and dramas on this town's dock area:
Long spun tangled webs found where tense figures work
And meet down piers; waves of trouble landing here.
Clash of force and feeling: hide deep poisons: that disembark.

A View From The Bridge, On The Waterfront. Anna Christie: sees
The shaft of light, love might cast on the dark scene,
Dockers enact through fist, blade, shots: to seize
Power from the far side: unjust states of lives have seen.

A port film on plague landing: named *Panic in The Streets*:
Predicts Corona Virus, causing wide alarm, today.
Black and White: this work located far across The States:
Reflects dark and light contrasts: Brooklyn shores can say.

The *French Connection* lands. Tough Cop Hackman: pursues
Dire imports in dope which can vastly kill.
This town holds fear: for its best case, or box-office take, to tell
The truth. A story, hot like hellfire, standing to lose.

A Virus Strain the Movies Own

At L.A. waves crash on shore. Wind bends crossed palms:
Hands shake to sign contracts: expanding aims
From rough street quarters. Lives turn to the stars:
High. handsome, plush. Until sheer illusion shatters.

Girls who serve diners. Tough guys digging cable lengths:
Snapped up by hawk-eyed film agents.
They'll need act no more, than move in their own sense.
Cameras like their style: sharply cut. So, the hit show runs.

Hitchcock: the great film man of menace and suspense.
Works on the line of *Spellbound, Vertigo, Psycho.*
Corona Virus: striking unseen, fatal beyond sense.
He could make such an epic, eerie: through soundtrack echo.

Film Noir: one virus: shook off by Hollywood.
A Touch of Evil, through: *Electra Glide*
In Blue: sped on up to: *Two Lane Black Top.*
Transports of sheer fright horror: the Movies might drop.

Weird fever of film-making itself: shows marked symptoms.
Sunset Boulevard, leads to *The Player*: sketched by Altman.
Psycho probes of ego mania: infect show-business terms.
Corona fears steal in: when Art House lights go down.

Rio Rich to the Rio Afar

Landing here, prior to reaching The Amazon:
And take a rough boat, long steaming to the source.
Could that Virus, or less troubles, seize upon
Lives urged to taste this savage remoteness?

At Rio: we'd climbed the Christ mount: Corcovado:
Which means, spine-twisted shape. Said of people who
Live in shack towns, called the Favela,
Where harsh weather and dirt debris, swirl through.

Hard to notice, when the Virus strikes pestilence:
The righteous sort, say each louche squatter deserves:
In pay-out for their unhygienic or godless sins.
Corona grips, worse than the ills, Job suffers.

On the Amazon: grand opera appears at Manaus
In the jungle. Launched by that wild film hero:
Fitzcarraldo, who canoed the cast of Bellini's
The Puritans. Right up here, to enact their show.

Based on Pilgrims who settled White America.
Staged in *The Crucible*. Witchcraft imagined rife.
Those accused falsely: denounced through jurist and vicar:
To be hanged. Each case: an innocent country wife.

Off the freight boat: we caught Pirhana.
Tasty, fried. The trick's to eat them sooner,
Than they'll eat you. Clouds break. Deluge falls massive.
Amid all that Corona fear, we must survive.

Isolate One Self

Strange, to be urged that way, when the social scene,
Lured one night and day: until the crisis came.
Pubs and all venues slam their doors.
Human contact risks: to spread this virus.

A life apart: once the lone preserve
Of the writer, sifting words to solve
Statements of debt or credit, in a live account
Of those to survive, or close sadly down to end.

Solitary state: marked by figures of renown.
The tough sort, hard to manage, locked in prison.
Real castaways, like Crusoe and Ben Gunn:
Or pretend types from the *Desert Discs* program.

Who pick tunes you hate. Best be left home alone.
Play a Bach Partita: a Chopin Nocturne.
Those I knew close: by other ways, have gone.
Wartime scarce kept us apart from each loved one.

Urban terror strikes: causing vigilant concern.
Virus threats, hide deeper. Science needs a solution.
Shores silent: waves ebb unseen under a hunter's moon.
Locked in from the wasted blazing sun:
We count ways where global troubles turn.

Secluded Matters

Held fast at home, while that virus prevails:
Warned that going out, risks to spread this germ,
And dare face penalty: defying urgent calls
To save this country, from deeper harm.

This mood: still, quiet, warm-cocooned;
While the world outside, might whirl to entice
Reminds of past states in off quarters, confined
Through limbs injured; or work ended, hard to lose.

No bright time outside, to miss. All switched out.
Dutch interiors silenced beyond power of words.
Finesse of girls, through deep shades, caught in shafts of light.
Or the hunted kind, hidden from Race-hating armed squads.

Another cause, when stayed slunk down one's becalmed den.
No urge to move the will to reason or to thrive.
"Death-Wish": a stasis in philosophy; sank down.
Meaning drained from steps forward, to act alive.

Retreats at the house, in still shell of the self:
Shadow lines drawn by a devout or mystic mode.
Probes through the skin, pierce an imagined life.
Inward versions of pilgrim routes: mark the vow made.

Pictured through concept, art, or writing, achieved:
Traits counter to wild impulse urged to acting out.
Mirroring restrained caution through past times we lived.
Enforced seclusion, forms chance moments to create.

Troubles Cross the Sea

In Dublin's dear city: talk flows like the Liffey.
Good to brew up the stout. The best pint to come out,
That loosens the tongue, when the long day is done.
Pulled up from the cellar; to wear a white collar.
Most soberly dressed, as a canny church priest.
Who'll hear you confess; moved by drastic duress.
To spill out your sins. But never drop once:
Taste for liquid black gold: not served warm or too cold.
As winter outside, storms the bleak Liffey side.
In statue, Molly Malone, still shivers alone.
A hungry, hand-clasping, brave poet, stands busking
Lines on snow-bound streets, found hard as W. B.Yeats.
I pay his small fee, for "The Lake Isle of Innisfree".
Out past the pub door, some drag on cig or cigar.
At the rooms inward, evil smoke is outlawed.
From bitter years since, crowds came to their sense.
Now this Corona Virus, creeps a speck unseen by us:
Shuts pubs right down. That great talk flown,
Fast as swallows reach Spain, our glasses must drain.
Walking far, banned also. So hard, knowing where to go:
But home with a stout six-pack, carried out safely back.
Switch on the radio, if there's anything left to know.
O'Casey's *Plough and the Stars*, makes a play on the wars.
That Easter Rising stand, to throw the English from the land.
This Corona Virus, the next damned thing.
Might also take one hell of a beating

Banking on a Safe Return

Staged like mid-life crisis, on country-wide scale:
Britain stalls, full stop. Closed brackets, long pause imposed.
The question mark. We'll end this soon? Lines call,
Fearing, Clause Four looks as if now being used.
Left Wing's dictum: the State must run vital means,
We live on. Transport, mines, steel plants. Health care,
The one most public owned: vied against private lines.
All joined up now, to face the Virus scare.

To starve disease from victim lives it thrives upon:
They're locked at home. Streets, schools, works, pubs: devoid.
Medic wards, all that's left now still running.
Ironic: health staff most risk infection feared.
Nursing times lend much to deep told drama.
Patients' last words, poignant. Carers, fallen: reft the heart
Of the land. Staff in their prime, lost. When this trauma
Strikes: firm-lipped kinds, all threats will thwart.

Past years, like this: when the land halted; now recalled.
Wartimes: all drawn close, kept the flame in common cause:
Endured harsh change in habit, custom and laws.
Blacked-out in curtained homes, so lives will not be killed.
Back then, commerce kept tight. Profit, free trade, held off.
Now, bare streets sense an unseen enemy to hate;
Stronger than armies: freezing up money and active life.
Will our free choice in wealth, return, wide: separate;
Or stay in that Clause, now ruling by The State.

Desert Island Blues

That sound-wave slot: long to cause sharp scorn
In lives at home; if choice made, not to their taste.
Now, Virus maroons us: one can enact alone,
Through endless music played where all are cast:

Each a monarch to survey a lone island: that John Donne
Built verse on: saying: we cannot live there.
Get off his own, devised part, and join the common main.
Smart lines meant lasting fame for that Holy Father.

A bell tolls for the sad lost, fallen to disease.
Wireless reports distress. Better, when a disc spins.
Locked down, remote, no one near to accuse:
You should be locked up, mad, to hoard such tunes.

In my case: extreme. Records bought six decades back,
Sound worn, misty: jolting old memories.
Before the surface of slick Pop, gross Punk, Hard Rock,
Great symphonies or Classic Jazz, haunted our days

Live crack in pubs, I miss. Or else lockdown could suit
My lifestyle: thought needing update, goes the word.
A desert island suspect: none in my chosen eight,
Moves far past Bach, Ravel, Kid Ory, Monk or Bird.

Palm Sunday Dropped Through Illness

Crowds hope forwards to this day: a date to mark again.
Ripe as fruit from the palms; that gave its name.
Those leaves, and coats, strewn across, to ease the path
For the Master, approaching: thought of great worth.

Virus scares, wipe this sacred day from the map.
How Zionists sweep Gaza left bank lives away;
Aiming to make that paused, palm-applauding city
Israel's capital: wealth and power, builds up

Christ-led souls: the third part here, hailing that power
Islam nor Israel: never move to share:
His creed for peace and equal social right.
No big deal for the venal, macho sort.

These divided ways, stretch to the end of the earth.
Which might fall soon, now Corona Virus bites in.
The Bible and more faiths, long speak of.
Rational sorts, crave a forensic solution.

In England: all grand occasions, now ruled out
Bare churches, as often: dust-blown and creaking.
On this day of triumph, no one may congregate.
Wide aisles, deserted. In choirs, none will sing.

Prayer that pleads the last chance: observed at home.
Plus hand-washing, and keeping six feet from one's spouse.
Some knowing such stance for decades in their house.
Making up for lost sins, looks running out of time.

The Last Deliverer rode a donkey here on earth.
A sign of care and peace, some leaders invent,
To fool the people over their dark intent.
The Nazarene, revered. The lone one to act the truth.

Gethsemane Visits Not Advised

Few days past Palm Sunday. Tributes, now stood down.
Same as sports events: they've turned to a virtual screen.
Gethsemane would follow. Now, a closed garden.
Virus scares, added to troubles, long ago.
To misquote words to bemused Malvolio:
Think not because you are now Virtual,
There shall be no more hot cakes and real ale.
This Bible act: long in doubt, might now become
Packaged, sold as a computer game.
Paired with The Ides of March, when Caesar came:
Aware as Christ, those whispered omens, mean
The end is near. Both cassettes bring a public warning.
Known in each real case. Betrayal: the vital piece
In each play: the presentiment of sacrifice.

In common lockdown at home. Art books open,
On great painters of that Garden scene.
From Caravaggio, El Greco, Goya to Gauguin:
Portrayed in garments of their own time, that recall,
Betrayals and executions, which raged still.
Back at Judea: stark moments, tomorrow, would fall.
Easter: we now count on from each rising moon.
Sentence begun from high cross nails drove home.
Touching sharp agony in Pasolini's raw film.
Corona Virus: called an evil anti-force let in,
From human waste, to corrupt, poison, by pollution.
Long echoed through deep lines by Yeats.
"What rough beast, its hour come round at last,
Slouches towards Bethlehem to be born?"

Dark Sides of Culture Blamed

A certain kind of person appears on earth:
From the start, shaping a stance to combat,
Pitfalls and perils of outrageous fortune,
Hamlet or Iago; portrayed as their mortal hurt.
Moved to disturb fine dust well settled.
Plagued by doubt. Pledged to avenge wrong sustained.

Some sort of trouble brews deep in the world:
A strain of culture: that toxic plants ferment:
To cure illness through remedy from past old ways.
Or in essence, to distil a spirit which inspires.
Or over-used, clouds judgement, distorts the will:
Unleashed, to threaten damage: aimed to kill.

Growths turned to opiates: inject false heights of perception.
Potions to poison, out of chance or sheer intent.
Unseen on earth, as powers possessed by virus.
Once, slipped in wine, causing a poisoned chalice:
Humans pass to others, by inhuman motives,
To claw back vengeance from vile flaws, blood sends down.

Byron and Shelley, wrote swift lines: launched to accuse masters,
Who exile them, remote as from a fever virus zone.
Byron started a revolt to free Greek people.
Shelley denounced evil outrage struck at Peterloo.
One poet dying from the bite of a mosquito.
The other hero, drowned in a stormed sea squall.

A century on:. Owen and Sassoon, brought a bleaker strain:
Met in a medic ward. Flesh wounds able to heal.
Symptoms in the head: harder to ease down.
Siegfried taught Wilfred: skills in anger of each poem;
Admired cricket's opening batsmen: Hobbs and Rhodes
Stoic, skilled, watchful, enduring as those soldier poets.

The game called off in wartime. Grounds fell silent.
Players in whites: turned khaki-clad on battlefields.
Their words changed, voicing anger, fierce as huge guns,
Against war: long, filthy, futile. Blaming distant powers.
For cause and reason hard to see. Now, this hidden Virus,
Spreads a sense of siege, descended all around.

Saving the Right Ending

To learn a trade or run a firm: never my aim.
Desk at school, stirred no taste for office, high or low.
A clerk's job: soon fled: to drift down the road.
Words written any place; dreamed up in my head,

Poet, I once put down, my trade, at a job centre.
"You'll take other things? Not much call for that here,"
The clerk said. Sure, I'd tried them all, anyway
In short spells, where the magic fast wears away.

Those I've known: honed skills, found work to build
Their own firm. Called the sort to gather moss:
Green as lucre. A rolling stone failed to grasp, wide across
The globe. Once, enticing from classrooms, recalled.

World credit, failing: hit all to the hilt: in debt:
Banking on neither. Void in a flat broke state:
Work dried up, I'd stick to the writing one.
Solved by staying in, juggling words, alone.

Now Virus fires at all lives: three lines of fate:
To die. Or lose all trade. To stay locked down.
The first, all hope to beat. The rest, to reclaim.
In a still house, waiting word of change to come.
Long my brief assigned: ordered well to write.
But for wider lives: I care for their outcome

Moonlight on Time Enclosed

Moonlight steals in, boldly daring.
Like a thief in the night, breaking in.
The house: still, in lockdown. No one
Allowed to call: in fear of Virus let in.
The moon, full faced, bright-eyed, most welcome,
In the dark night of the sole occupant
Of the house not yet paid for, A last refuge.
As that art painting "Raft of The Medusa" meant.
Survivors of a wreck, striving where storms rage.

The moon that levels tides: a lamp by our door.
Broad beams, build assurance in each room.
Through silence: lilts from piano keys, incite
One to discern that sonata called, "The Moonlight".
The person who played this instrument, now gone.
Their ghost not back for a last encore, this time.

The radio emits that work by Beethoven.
Marking time on the year when he was born.
Moving on to play his Eroica, and Fifth Symphony.
Hard pressed notes, evoking war and destiny.
Lastly, "Ode to Joy", in his jubilant setting,
Lifts spirits, which fight the Virus, raging on.

Shadows in the Smoke

From shadows he'll lurch: first unseen, then sharply there
At your elbow that crooks to raise a drinking glass.
Pert as vermin: more quaint, comic: his manner.
Small in stature. A mask moulded to wide roles, his face.

To sense you've known before: part of his luring charm.
None near his sort, amid crowds mingling.
Bright cheer which drowns out the threat of harm;
Sweeps aside instinct that should alarm a warning.

Gaining confidence: name of the game played both sides.
Your nervous steps, needing advance from solitude.
His easy move to a free blank space; that hides
Tactics thought to control across the board.

This pub in fact an old train coach on the street
By the line where it used to speed lives in and out,
Up or down: all ways he knows prepared to meet
Each minute chance turns moves clear from doubt.

Games played in this rail pub, will edge his keen
Wits practised on the cards, dice, dominoes.
Your number comes up. Virus the last one
Nightmare to miss: for lives held sheer in the balance.

Black Country Codes

Past huge cities: still this terrain won't find
Grass, trees, pretty views: beyond iron works.
The Black Country sifts honest dirt through cracks,
In a hundred trades that build and mend the land.

Reckless Dan deals in scrap, A price drummed up for each
Item carted to tips. Recycled, nothing lost.
All waste finds homes some place, to pitch
Up in another guise, at further cost.

Each rough town runs into the next. Yet stays distinct
In name and trade, it peddles, to keep alive.
That nasal accent alters slight in sound.
Hard to glean through tastes of biting wit they leave.

Dan slammed down the nick once: dealing motors called hot.
If he knew or not: no scrap of difference:
When The Law rules out of order, goods that fence
From one rogue to the next, who haggle and tot.

Low in stealth, blind as that Virus can creep in:
Most contacts made by distancing
From trouble brewed. No handshake given.
Wash your hands from all that dark suspicion.
Trade at home, safe, still to make a living,

Close of Play

North Leeds looks close knit: hard as grit to find.
Breweries make that most dry, bitter taste.
Yeadon Airport: most high and windswept in the land.
Flies to Ulster and Poland. Nowhere that sounds tourist.

Headingley Cricket Ground: knew tough games to win.
Close and Verity: raised in streets around:
Nearest you'll find for true zest to gain.
Found here, sent far, by Yorks and England.

Bradman hit huge fast hundreds here four times.
Rhodes and Sutcliffe plundered runs from this turf.
Trueman or Lindwall knocked stumps far off.
This ground a harsh test for robust teams.

Not this year. Virus spin bowled out the fixture list.
Stands, empty. Eyes at home: glint on a summer lost.
Up Yorkshire's Stand, the Honours Board now missed
Chance to write up a hundred scored or five wicket haul:
Where heroes leave their mark written tall.

Only ground staff brooding in this empty place,
Scan those legends and the blank scoreboard today.
Lives lost or in fear from strains of Virus.
Verity played till 1939. Then, shot in Sicily
Lives most vital, struck down by war or disease:
Cricket holds a poignant view on the close of play.

Words for a Cabinet Briefing

Keen, the backbencher grasps that urge for power,
Though an unseen bug now starts from The East.
Stirring China, Japan, Vietnam, Korea:
Who all waged wars in decades past, at huge cost.
Other conflicts since; come back to roost:
As though global reproof resurges at this hour.

Elected to office: no time of a calm, easy brief.
Death toll and social stasis, harsh as war, now brings.
Flimsy as a Munich Paper, shaking like a leaf:
Jargon uttered, figures quoted: to hope balance,
This tightrope act: anxious to relieve,
Tension on which the fate of nations hangs.

Good times to bury the worst news:
Tactics used, to govern, in a safer phase:
Could reverse now, in this state of Virus.
Horror shielded, by the stock glib phrase.
"Ramp up testing. Stay safe. Lockdown": The call,
This spokesman employs: in looking the most cool.

Grave Reflection

Amid the Virus crisis and harsh toll
To sound the names and heavy numbers gone,
In action of the clapper upon the bell,
Starkly graphic and tonal in outcome,
Stunned by word coming: of one taken.
Pause for breath, on the cusp of silence,
Before the church rings sound like doom.

Reflects on one self, who mirrors that plain life
Wrenched from wide ranks in this random cull.
Old age, road crash, heart-failure, suicide,
Not the cause: but force unseen, unjust as evil
Mounted like famine, massacre: grave omens said,
Lead to the plague that wreaks revenge past belief.

From this loss, a short step to the graveyard near:
Often to visit, by the white stones carved
For those fallen in the stages of World War,
Acts struck from the sea and sky, through alien fear.
Though wrongs count up: sheer conflict, derived
From nature distorted, we know no answer for.

Inquest Postponed

A patient case just expired on the table:
Stretched to list masses swift and sadly gone.
Art and text glimpse vast losses back to The Ark
Which plucked pairs of each creature from wide flood:
Claims of insurance call an act of god, that name
In dispute, where virus reminds divides of old.

When miracles cured disaster. Back to square one
No belief or doubt, able to decipher, this time.
When human error pled aware: wrecking the sphere:
Out of guilt, pledged measures to restore.
Strange, how creatures escape this scourge struck down.
A force to equal rights, unleashing from
The balance to account: final judgement, to come.

Mebyon Kernow Bells Ring

Church bells sound far and wide by radio,
Pealed from that finger of land pointing out
Where west wind brings fear or hope to Kernow.
That name in Cornish their own tongue spells out.

Few words I knew, sworn in and enrolled
By the zealot farmer, I worked times for
On this land, the first and last county, they called.
Home rule long resounding through the keen moist air,

In the song pledged to uphold Trelawney,
Marching to break England's grasping fist.
Words by Parson Hawker. Coroner of the sea,
For those drowned on this fierce coast.

Clung to the sense of a distinct Celt blood:
He drank opium to stand times he must recognise
Bodies distorted by storm tides huge in flood,
Pitiless as Virus strikes each innocent who dies.

Rage hoped to be passing: now bells ring.
To reflect how war longed for peace to come
Now stand for peals that mark a plague going
Counting out those lost to tolls beaten in the storm.

Plaid Cymru Find Their Cure

Out on a limb from mainstream thought, to imagine,
Joining outcasts, together, acting free
In time of study round West Wales, urged begin
To scan between the devil of fierce wind blowing
And wrecks of distrust cast down the deep blue sea

My teacher worked best, talking in the bar room;
Steeped in dissent which shaped those acute fells.
In his head, a library for well-versed thought to roam
Across each wit-laced patch of doubt-torn Wales.

Harlech Castle's dead tooth: Gaunt as a scar.
In *Richard the Second*: a named character,
Listing lost Anglo values, in declined litany:
"This realm, a precious stone set in a silver sea."

Fury on both sides, that a vacation cottage burn.
Or Welsh in shops, voice sudden their old tongue:
Lashed out rare to scorn visits of those alien,
Before Virus lockdown: deep inured to distancing.
Keeping loss down over sparse fell and frozen tarn

Skye Home Address

First time we met where a Glasgow pub's sharp tones
Rang like old tills taking beer cash; or the bells
Tolled closing time when uproar swells and drones
Huge as the Clyde where vast hope builds and falls.

And gave me his address curt as a Gorbals crack
Sends wit fast from the tongue or blows from the fist.
He'll ship out from this clamour, past a snowy creek,
Where glen and shore hold another moving feast.

Found now, in true nature, on the Isle of Skye.
At a croft hovel, where to write and paint
Outlines of clouds that shape faces passing by,
Caught briefly, let go: as kites or doves are sent.

At Skye's vast sheer blue: we cannot hold belief,
This place owned by grey church, counting house or throne.
Vile as sharks, like Virus threats to life.
Clouds cleanse the air. Released senses moving on

Escape at Enniskillen

A lady, ninety years old, at Enniskillen;
Caught, but survived, cured, from the virus strain.
A tribute to brave health care given,
And to being resistant in this terrain,
I've known: close to the tense split border line
Through Ulster; that keeps sides apart: who lean
To the orange flag or to the green:
Where Anglo values slid between.

Four hundred years, draining that vein
Of dividing: where the aloof can gain
Land, wealth, kudos: imperial traits bring.
Till 1926: when fragile settlement came.
In '69, Burntollet burst out rage, to open
Trouble brewed long: fired huge again,
To a dog-kill-dog campaign:
Turned worse, as mad barking came.
Killing near more than virus would claim.

Just down the road from Granddad's farm:
All the same green stretched country then.
His daughter had lived to reach ninety-one:
Equal to this lady, now nine decades on.
Famed wide for beating this Virus strain:
As some longed to break that grip on Eireann.
Aunt Rebecca nearing the end of her time
Told me of days when Eire lived as one;
Glad to catch her last moment's gleam:
And hear now, this lady's escape at Enniskillen.